A TIME FOR REFLECTION

A TIME FOR REFLECTION

Talks for Secondary School Assemblies

Derek James

Book Guild Publishing
Sussex, England

First published in Great Britain in 2009 by
The Book Guild Ltd
Pavilion View
19 New Road
Brighton, BN1 1UF

Typesetting in Garamond by
Nat-Type, Cheshire

Printed in Great Britain by
CPI Antony Rowe

A catalogue record for this book is available from
The British Library.

ISBN 978 1 84624 294 6

*To my mother, who made many
sacrifices for my education.*

Contents

CONTENTS

TALKS FOR SIXTH-FORM ASSEMBLIES

Introduction

If you are like me, you will be slightly irritated whenever you are expected to read an introduction before getting down to the 'meat' of a book you have chosen. If I am not bored by it, as I frequently am, I am nevertheless likely to become impatient with something that is delaying me from getting down to reading what I want to read. On top of that, I sometimes feel that the writer is trying to mould my thoughts so that I read the book as he or she intended. I prefer to gain my own impressions first and only then read what the author was trying to do; judge for myself his or her success and possibly revise my own opinion in the light of the author's aims. I therefore recommend that you stop reading this introduction now and perhaps return to it after you have finished the book, or, at least, as much of it as holds your interest.

I toyed with the idea of placing the introduction at the end of the book, but rejected it as too gimmicky. In this case there is an additional reason for reading the introduction last: the book is a collection of talks given in assemblies. The students had no introduction, not even a short one; they had to hear the talk 'cold' and make up their own minds about it – or not bother, as the case may be. It seems preferable, therefore, that the reader is in the same position.

* * *

Assuming that you have taken my advice and have now read at least some of the talks, I shall explain briefly my motives and a few of my thoughts on school assemblies.

Most of the talks are my recollection of those I gave between 1990 and 2003 in assemblies at Westminster City School. A few I did not give, but would do if I were still teaching. The school is an inner London comprehensive, boys only from Years 7 to 11, but with a mixed Sixth Form. It is not a church school; however, entrants and their parents do have to accept its Christian ethos. They do not all have to be Christian but, at least in Year 6 or 7, they will have a connection with either a church, mosque or temple, for example. I mention this to acknowledge that it was easier to talk about religious matters in assembly than it would be in some schools. Many teachers are, nevertheless, unnecessarily hesitant about touching on religious issues. Far more youngsters than one might expect – whatever the school – are interested in religious ideas as long as they are not presented in a naïve, childish way.

Having taught for 38 years in secondary schools, I have sat through a great number of assemblies. When I was a pupil myself the pattern of them was unvarying – a hymn, a prayer and a short bible reading. I would not denigrate that; in fact I like set liturgy and ritual; however, I accept that it would be hard to make it work well today. I am sure that some of the best assemblies, certainly the most enjoyable ones, are those that involve pupil participation, drama or music. Not all of us can manage that successfully, and, in any case, there should be occasions for experienced adults to present their thoughts on and insights into life, to which students have to listen. Otherwise, what is the point of experience, or indeed of school?

The problem is, or at least has been in my experience, that at least half of the talks are fairly boring and make morning assembly a dreaded part of the day for many students. Before 1990, most of my assemblies would have fallen into this category. I wince when I remember some of the tasteless fare I dished up. I would say that there are five or six reasons for assembly talks being boring or, even if they are not boring, of no real value to hundreds of teenagers who, quite rightly, resent having their time wasted.

If the speaker lacks confidence, this is obviously a disadvantage. Most of us probably feel nervous the first time we take an assembly and we should improve the more we lead. In any case, even teenagers can give nervous teachers a fair chance if they are being sincere. If they are speaking or reading about some high moral principle that they clearly do not believe, or do not act by, it will soon become evident. In this connection, I would say that it is nearly always better to speak your thoughts rather than read them, which does not come across as so genuine. I used to prepare what I wanted to say in my head and rehearse it several times so that I had it almost off pat, but I never wrote it down.

It is important for the talk not to go on too long; five or ten minutes is ample. After that, an increasing number of students are going to start thinking about other things. Many clergymen do not seem to appreciate this. If their sermon goes on for more than 20 minutes, they will have undone all the good they did in the first five. Another fault of theirs to avoid, is to ensure that the same point is not driven home again and again. Any teacher knows that youngsters forget things and need to be reminded of them many times; however, not in the same assembly. Once at the beginning and once at the end should be more than enough.

There are many people and events that students should know about and that are good, and easy, subjects for assemblies, because they are important, because they lend themselves to good moral advice and because they are safe, in the sense that no decent person is likely to be offended or feel uncomfortable about what is said. For those very reasons, however, students may have already had many assemblies about them. With the best will in the world it is hard not to think 'not her again' when you realise you are about to sit through your tenth assembly on Florence Nightingale.

This leads naturally to my last, and most heartfelt, criticism of so many school assemblies. To 'play it safe' many speakers have avoided anything challenging and have stuck to commonplace ideas and platitudes that youngsters have heard over and over again. In my experience, teenagers can grasp, or at least grapple with, difficult or unusual ideas and prefer something that makes them think to the endless 'dumbing down' of assemblies, that often really say no more than 'be good' or 'work hard' many times over.

The words 'be good' remind me of another sort of ghastly assembly – the nag. Boys being boys, children being children, this will sometimes be necessary; however, it should be very rare, as it will mean it is impossible to make the assembly uplifting or interesting, and will reinforce the impression that assemblies are among those things that nobody likes but school makes compulsory.

In the talks in this book I tried to avoid the weaknesses I have just listed. Above all, I tried to make the students think. At times I made an off-the-cuff remark that I hoped would make some of them smile, or even result in a 'friendly'/sarcastic teenage groan, but I never paused or drew attention to these in case they did not work. Few things backfire in an assembly more than an obvious attempt at humour, unless you know you are good at it. It is not for me to say whether or not my assemblies succeeded, but I felt happy at the end of each of them and I was often complimented on them by students as well as staff. One student even told me some years after leaving school, that my assemblies were the only ones he remembered.

I have written this book to show the sort of talks, the sort of topics, which went down reasonably well with inner-city, secondary-age students. I do not recommend that anyone reads them or recites them in an assembly. If you think some of the ideas are worth repeating, I would suggest that you make them your own by composing your own assembly talk around them.

GENERAL AND MORAL
TALKS

Lighting a Candle

There is an old saying that I think is both very true and very valuable: 'It is better to light a single candle than to curse the darkness.' I'll repeat it by way of emphasis: 'It is better to light a single candle than to curse the darkness.'

As well as, of course, being literally true, it is, as I'm sure many of you have already realised, meant to be understood metaphorically: it is better to do one good deed, however small, than to curse or grumble at how bad things are.

I expect many of you already know the truth of this from your own experience. You must know some people who are always moaning but never do anything that makes a difference, and others who quietly get on with little things and bring about an improvement. There are many famous people in history, especially the saints, whose individual acts have changed things enormously for the better. I'm not going to talk about any of them however, but about two far more obscure people.

The first is a lady called Dora, who told her story on Radio 4 some years ago. She lived on a large estate in south London that was really rundown. Damage, rubbish and graffiti were everywhere in the grim-looking flats; gangs of youths loitered about the place, looking menacing; old people were afraid to go out at night. Dora had already been burgled twice. She had no doubt which group of teenagers was responsible, but she had no proof and didn't want to be laughed at and insulted, or

3

worse, by accusing them. Then her flat was broken into a third time, and this time the thieves stole her prized collection of '78' records. That may not mean much to you in these days of CDs and iPods, but many people a little older than me used to be very attached to their 78 rpm records. They were Dora's favourite possessions and she decided to do something instead of just moaning, however little prospect there seemed of it doing much good.

She went up to the group she was certain had broken in, told them what she thought of them and explained how much the records meant to her. Within a few days the records were returned, but the effect of what she had done went far beyond that. The youths started to talk to her, saying how bored they were, how there was nothing to do and nowhere to go. Dora managed to get a community hall on the estate opened up for them to meet in (it had been shut for years because of lack of interest and vandalism). Before long she involved other adults in helping her to run a youth club there.

It began to make a difference to the whole atmosphere on the estate. Dora was elected to the management committee and later on to the local council, which she persuaded to spend money on improving the estate, including large structural improvements. Within a few years the estate had changed from being one nobody wanted to move into and everyone wanted to leave, to the exact opposite. And it had all started when one person made a small, individual stand instead of just grumbling; when she lit a single candle.

The second person I want to mention achieved no such dramatic results. One morning I took a telephone call in my office from a member of the public. She started by saying, 'I want to talk to you about one of your boys.' Any teacher will appreciate why at that moment my heart sank, because people only ever phone in to complain that boys have been rowdy on the bus, fighting in the street, swearing in the shops ... but this time it was different.

The lady said that she'd been waiting at a bus stop when her friend, another elderly lady, collapsed unconscious. No one helped her. People walked past pretending they hadn't noticed, or looked sympathetic but glanced at their watches as they hurried on, as if to say that they'd like to assist but didn't have the time. Then a small boy in our uniform came along and guessed that the lady was diabetic and needed some sugar quickly (his nan had the same complaint). He rushed into a nearby sweetshop, bought some boiled sweets and put a couple into the lady's mouth. She revived and it would be nice to say that the boy had saved her life. However, he hadn't. An ambulance soon arrived, summoned by a nearby shopkeeper who had seen the lady collapse. In any case, diabetics generally carry a few lumps of sugar with them, as the lady's friend would probably have remembered once she'd recovered from her panic. So I suppose you could say that the boy need not have bothered; he could have saved his money and not made himself late for school. But I wouldn't say that. He saw a bad situation, he knew there was one thing he could do to improve it and he did exactly that. I doubt whether God asks more than that from most of us.

30 January

As both a student and teacher of history, I take notice of dates and anniversaries. Today, 30 January, is the anniversary of at least four significant events, each of them, in my opinion, bad.

30 January 1972 is known as Bloody Sunday, when British soldiers fired on demonstrators in Northern Ireland, killing 13 of them. Whatever the rights and wrongs of the action, it certainly left a legacy of resentment and hatred. Many innocent people were to die in the years to follow.

On 30 January 1948 Mahatma Gandhi was shot and killed. He had led the people of India in their campaign for independence from Britain, always insisting on non-violence and using only peaceful means of protest and obstruction. When, after independence was achieved, fighting broke out between Hindus and Muslims, he tried to bring peace and understanding and was shot by a fellow Hindu who regarded him as a traitor. Gandhi's example has inspired many other people to adopt his methods in campaigning for causes they believe in.

On 30 January 1933 Adolf Hitler became Chancellor of Germany and began the 12 years of what he called the Third Reich. Hitler was about as different from Gandhi as anyone could be: he believed that might is right. There was no right or wrong, only struggle and force, and the most ruthless would – and should – prevail. Some 50 million people died because of him.

Much further back in time, on 30 January 1649, King Charles I was executed. His impact on history has been less than either Gandhi's or Hitler's; however he is the person I am going to speak about.

Charles I aroused strong feelings in his own age and has done so ever since. Historians disagree over whether he was a good man or a bad man, a good king or a bad king, and many politicians have regarded themselves as heirs of his supporters or his opponents. Today, as every year, people will lay flowers at the foot of his statue in Whitehall, near the spot where he was beheaded. The Church of England commemorates him as a martyr – someone who dies for what he or she believes in – and there are even a few churches dedicated to King Charles the Martyr. King Charles believed so firmly in the monarchy and the Church of England that he would not compromise his beliefs to save his life. I admit that I'm one of his admirers, but to be fair to his detractors, a dreadful civil war occurred in his reign, so I suppose you could say that he failed in the most important task of a king – to preserve the unity of his people. Nearly everyone, however, whether they think he lived well or not, will agree that he died well. His death is one of the two things I want to draw your attention to.

Charles had lost the civil war and had been given what might pass as a trial by his enemies. He was declared guilty of treason and of making war on his people and was condemned to death. Kings had been killed in battle before or even murdered secretly, but no English king had ever been executed publicly, so it was a dramatic event. Charles was perfectly calm, said goodbye to his younger children (the older ones and his wife had escaped abroad), took Holy Communion and walked out of his palace of Whitehall to the platform erected for his beheading. It was a very cold morning and he put on two shirts.

He didn't want to shiver from the cold in case people thought he feared death, which he did not. Thousands of people had come to watch and hundreds of soldiers formed a barrier between them and the king in case any of them tried to rescue him. One of the soldiers said 'God bless Your Majesty' as he walked past and was smacked on the head with a musket by his sergeant.

When Charles was on the scaffold he was allowed to say a few words to the people, and he gave a purse of money and his blessing to the executioner to show that he did not blame him for doing his job. He put his head on the block and held his hands forward. In one he held a handkerchief, explaining that he wanted to say a few prayers and would drop the handkerchief when he had finished as a sign to the executioner to strike. I think that in his place I'd have suddenly remembered a lot of very long prayers to delay the moment, but Charles was brief and his head came off with one blow. A witness recalled that when the executioner held it up there was such a groan from the crowd as he had never heard before and hoped never to hear again. Charles had died with such courage and dignity that within days he was being referred to as a martyr. By dying so well he helped to bring about the eventual victory of what he had seemed to lose. Parliament had abolished both the monarchy and the Church of England, yet only 11 years later both were restored when Charles's eldest son was invited to return and ascend the throne. Both, as you know, have survived to this day.

The other thing I want to draw your attention to is what Charles said at the opening of his trial a few days before his execution. This is much less dramatic but in some ways even more important. Parliament set up a special court to try the king. It wasn't like any other court with a judge and a jury; there were about 60 men to try him, none of them a real judge, but chosen because they were known to oppose him. Some were lawyers, some were MPs, some army officers, but the dominant figure was Oliver Cromwell. When the king was brought into court and the charges against him had been read out, its president – a man called Bradshaw – asked him how he pleaded. This still happens today, and the accused person says 'guilty' or, more usually, 'not guilty'. No doubt Bradshaw and the others expected Charles to say 'not guilty', but he didn't. Nor did he say 'guilty'. He simply asked what authority the court had to try him. Bradshaw could not give an answer because he knew the court had no lawful authority. Legally no court could try the king and legally that particular 'court' could not try anyone. So the king sat silent throughout the rest of the so-called trial.

It is worth quoting some of the king's actual words to Bradshaw, taken from C.V. Wedgewood's *The Trial of Charles the First*:

> I would know by what power I am called hither … I would know by what authority, I mean lawful; there are many unlawful authorities in the world, there are robbers and highwaymen … Let me know by what lawful authority am I seated here, and I shall not be unwilling to answer …
>
> [I would be betraying] that duty I owe to God and my country, if I were to submit to a tyrannical or any other ways unlawful authority … For if power without law may make laws, may alter the fundamental law of the kingdom, I do not know what subject he is in England that can be sure of his life.

In that last sentence, I would say the king put his finger on a fundamental principle of a civilised society: authority has to be lawful and not just based on force, on the power of the sword. If force alone rules you slide into barbarism, into either anarchy or tyranny, or more likely both in turn. In a way it is the same problem that faces us in the playground if a bully tells us to do something we don't want to do, or in the street if a mugger demands our money. It may, of course, be the case that the matter isn't important enough to risk being beaten up over, and we all hope we shan't be faced with a life and death issue like Charles I. However, every time we say 'no' to unlawful force we notch up a small victory for civilisation, and every time we give in to it we hand a victory to the terrible doctrine that 'might is right'.

Courage

A few days ago I was thinking about the qualities that are important in making someone a good human being; qualities like honesty, loyalty, kindness and perseverance to name a few. I wrote them down and before long I had a list of over 20. Then I began to consider which was the most important. The three great Christian virtues are faith, hope and love, of which the greatest is love. Far be it for me to disagree with St Paul. However, putting those to one side for the moment, I think the most important is courage. The reason is that courage has to support, underpin, all the other virtues. If it doesn't, they will all have their breaking point; they cannot be completely relied on.

Let me explain what I mean. Suppose a man is very kind to animals – a very good quality to have – and he sees someone ill treating one. If he has courage he will say or do what he can to help the animal; if he doesn't have courage he will fear what may happen to him if he gets involved and so he'll leave the animal to its fate. His kindness to animals has reached its breaking point; it hasn't produced any fruit. The same would apply to people who are very truthful, another really important quality. If they do not also have courage, then once it becomes dangerous to tell the truth, they'll tell a lie. I think it is the same with all the other virtues, even with faith, hope and love. Unless they are underpinned by courage – both physical and moral – they cannot ultimately be relied on.

Some time ago I listened to a Radio 4 play about Britain's prime minister during the Second World War, Winston Churchill. He was a man of great physical and moral courage all his life and is one of my heroes. During the broadcast the actor playing his character recited a poem that I had never heard before, but which greatly impressed me. So much so that I went to a good bookshop and searched through the poetry section until I found it. Over the next couple of weeks I did something I had not done since I'd had to do it as a schoolboy: I learnt a poem by heart. (To go off at a tangent for a moment, I strongly recommend that you all learn a favourite poem by heart. Far from being bored, I found that each time I read or recited the poem I enjoyed it more.)

The poem is called '*Invictus*', which is Latin for 'Unconquered' and it is by W.E. Henley. I imagine he was very ill or dying when he wrote it. I would not commend all the ideas in it – there is no hint of Christian hope or mercy or humility. However, we should hardly expect one poem to say everything we believe in. What Henley does show is an uncomplaining acceptance of personal responsibility and a great deal of courage. His courage ensures that he is unconquered whatever happens to him. Just one word of explanation: in the last verse the word 'strait' is not what we mean by straight. It's an old word meaning narrow. It alludes to the idea of the gate into heaven being narrow and difficult to get through, perhaps too difficult for W.E. Henley. I am going to recite the poem from memory, though I admit that I have a copy of it in my pocket in case my mind goes blank. Perhaps that shows a lack of courage on my part.

Out of the night that covers me,
Black as the pit from pole to pole,

I thank whatever gods may be
For my unconquerable soul.

In the fell clutch of circumstance
I have not winced nor cried aloud,
Under the bludgeonings of chance
My head is bloody, but unbowed.

Beyond this place of wrath and tears
Looms but the horror of the shade,
And yet the menace of the years
Finds, and shall find, me unafraid.

It matters not how strait the gate,
How charged with punishment the scroll,
I am the master of my fate:
I am the captain of my soul.

I'd like to end this assembly with my favourite prayer, composed by another brave man, but one who combined his courage with a strong Christian faith. He spent his early life as a soldier and then devoted himself to serving God and the Church. His name is St Ignatius Loyola, the founder of the Jesuits. The prayer is one we would all do well to repeat every day, though it will take courage to 'live' it:

Teach us, good Lord, to serve Thee as Thou deservest,
To give, and not to count the cost,
To fight, and not to heed the wounds,
To toil, and not to seek for rest,
To labour, and not to ask for any reward
save that of knowing that we do Thy will.

Amen

What Makes a Man?

When I was about 13 I read a tribute in my school magazine to a former pupil who had died. I had never known the man, but I was very impressed by a sentence in the tribute, which was a quotation from Shakespeare's *Julius Caesar* (Act V, Scene 5). This is the sentence:

> His life was gentle, and the elements
> So mixed in him that Nature might stand up
> And say to all the world, 'This was a man!'

I thought he must have been a wonderful person and I have remembered the words ever since. I've always thought that if I had to speak or write about a really fine man who had died, I might use them. Fortunately I haven't been called upon to do so, and I'm not sure that I've known anyone who would fully merit such a tribute. After all, you'd have to be quite something to be regarded as everything a man is meant to be. And what is a man meant to be?

To digress for just a moment, it may be that, although this is a boys' school, what I've already said is sounding sexist and old-fashioned. Why didn't I say 'person' or 'man/woman'? I don't want to get into that whole discussion now, but I would urge you not to let your views on this topic, however strong and principled they are, cut you off from a larger part of our literature and culture. Much of it has been male-centred and much of it uses 'man' to mean man or woman and 'he' to mean he or she. In fact in Anglo-Saxon, from which modern English is derived in the main, the word 'man' meant a human of either sex. If you discount or try to rewrite our cultural heritage, even with the best of intentions, you will lose more than you gain.

So then, what is a man meant to be? I thought about this for a few minutes, but soon realised that I could not put it better than it was put some 80 or more years ago by Rudyard Kipling in a poem called 'If'. It is one of the nation's favourite poems, so you may have heard it already. However, it is one of those poems that mean more each time you hear it, so I shall recite it now:

> If you can keep your head when all about you
> Are losing theirs and blaming it on you;
> If you can trust yourself when all men doubt you,
> But make allowance for their doubting too;
> If you can wait and not be tired of waiting,
> Or being lied about, don't deal in lies,
> Or being hated don't give way to hating,
> And yet don't look too good, nor talk too wise:
>
> If you can dream – and not make dreams your master;
> If you can think – and not make thoughts your aim;
> If you can meet with Triumph and Disaster
> And treat those two impostors just the same;
> If you can bear to hear the truth you've spoken
> Twisted by knaves to make a trap for fools,
> Or watch the things you gave your life to, broken,
> And stoop and build 'em up with worn-out tools:

If you can make one heap of all your winnings
And risk it on one turn of pitch-and-toss,
And lose, and start again at your beginnings
And never breathe a word about your loss;
If you can force your heart and nerve and sinew
To serve your turn long after they are gone,
And so hold on when there is nothing in you
Except the Will which says to them: 'Hold on!'

If you can talk with crowds and keep your virtue,
Or walk with kings – nor lose the common touch,
If neither foes nor loving friends can hurt you,
If all men count with you, but none too much;
If you can fill the unforgiving minute
With sixty seconds' worth of distance run,
Yours is the Earth and everything that's in it,
And which is more – you'll be a Man, my son!

If you can learn – this is not another verse of the poem, by the way, this is me again – if you can learn the whole poem by heart, do so; you'll find it very rewarding. If that seems too daunting, you could easily learn two lines or four. If I had to choose the four lines that I think are the most important, and thus the four I recommend that you learn, they would be these:

If you can force your heart and nerve and sinew
To serve your turn long after they are gone,
And so hold on when there is nothing in you
Except the Will which says to them: 'Hold on!'

What those four lines say is surely the basis of courage, determination, perseverance, strength of will, loyalty perhaps – the qualities that form the core of what we mean by manliness.

Sport

What I am going to talk about today has nothing to do with religion or morals or history, the subjects I usually tackle in assembly. I am going to say something about sport. I know there are some of you who do not like sport, who hate games afternoons and who try to persuade your mums to write notes to get you excused. I hope you won't stop listening however, as this talk is particularly aimed at you. Not only you, but mainly you.

Most of you know that I teach sport on two afternoons a week and, perhaps that I do some running, some sailing and a lot of walking in the mountains. I am very much in favour of sport; but it was not always so. When I was in primary school I did not like participating, except in swimming which I've always enjoyed. Football, cricket, boxing, gymnastics – they were all compulsory and I was not good at any of them. I was so bad at cricket that I was refereed to as 'tip it and run': if ever I managed to hit the ball even a few feet, I was so pleased with myself that I started to run, leaving the other batsman to be stumped out. At secondary school things were not much better for the first two years. The only time I scored a goal in football was when the teacher organised a special game for all the boys who were pretty useless. Even he referred to us a 'the scraps', which was a bit insulting, but at least we all had a chance.

Then everything changed. I was very lucky that at the

17

beginning of the third year – what we now call Year 9 – we were given the choice of continuing with normal games: a term each of football, athletics and cricket, or taking rowing for the whole year. I chose rowing, mainly to escape from the other three, but also because I had always liked boats and water. Anyway, I really enjoyed rowing and became reasonably good at it. I got into the school crews – eventually the first eight – and competed against other schools. I went to fitness training in the lunch break. Not only did I become a keen rower, my whole attitude towards sport changed. I rowed at university, joined a rowing club for a few years afterwards, then took up canoeing and sailing, which have remained lifelong interests. I have done a little caving and rock climbing, and a great deal of walking.

When I was about 35 another change took place. Some prefects suggested a ten-mile sponsored run for charity. I thought the idea ridiculous; I'd never run more than two or three miles and never really enjoyed it. However, I was persuaded and ran quite well. I became very keen, entered a number of races, including half-marathons and marathons, and derive a lot of pleasure and fitness from running to this day.

I am sorry to have spoken so much about myself, but I wanted to show how someone not interested in sport can become very keen on it if he or she finds an activity they like. Maybe there is a sport that you would love if you tried it. My advice to all those who do not like sport, is to try a new sport if you have the chance. If you don't like that, try another one. I suppose you cannot go on forever trying new sports, and I suppose some people will never like any. Of course, that is their right and they are no worse for it. There are many other things in life apart from sport. However, I have no doubt that regular, strenuous exercise is good for most people's physical and mental health, for their self-confidence and for an optimistic outlook on life.

For those of you who already enjoy sport, my advice is to continue with it after you leave school. As you grow older there will be many new demands on your time and attention, and it will be all too easy to give up sport and serious exercise. Many people who show real promise and talent at school end up having no more involvement with sport than what they can watch on television from an armchair, unable even to run 100 yards for a bus. The easiest way to maintain your interest is to join a sports club, but if that isn't possible do something with friends or by yourself. One of the great things about running is that you can do it more or less anywhere, by yourself or with others, with the minimum of equipment and organisation.

I think it is one of the old public schools that has the splendid Latin motto: *Mens sana in corpore sano.* It means 'A healthy mind in a healthy body'. This is a very good aspiration for all of us to have.

Dare to Be a Daniel

I expect you have all been given advice at various times not to be awkward or argumentative, not to spoil things, to cooperate, to be more agreeable. That is all good advice, which I would agree with – for the most part. But not always. Today I am going to give you the opposite advice and say that sometimes you should not go along with everyone else, sometimes you should dig your heels in and stand alone.

Until the 1970s, popes used to have a coronation at the beginning of their time in office, their reigns or pontificates as we say. It was a splendid affair in St Peter's Cathedral in Rome. Afterwards, the pope was carried around the great square outside at shoulder height in his special chair, called a *sedelia*. There would be numerous clergy in their best robes and crowds of people clapping and cheering. At three points as the pope – regarded as the most important person on earth by millions – was being carried around, a Franciscan friar would step in front of him and set fire to a bunch of flax in his hand. As it burnt he said to the pope *'Sic transit gloria mundi'*, which is Latin for 'Thus passes the glory of the world'.

It was a very graphic warning to the pope not to let all his new status and splendour, power and popularity go to his head, for one day it would all disappear as surely as the flax was disappearing in front of his eyes. I've never been able to understand why the Catholic Church abolished that little ceremony. Even if they thought a coronation was no longer appropriate, they could have kept that. In fact, I think it would be good for some similar act to be done before every monarch or president or prime minister, and not only them – before film stars, pop stars, sports celebrities, headmasters. It would not actually be a bad idea for us all to say it to ourselves at various times. The friar was not being a spoil-sport by standing apart from everyone else; he was giving an important lesson in keeping things in perspective.

A few years after stopping this ceremony, the Church abolished a position that I think was even more valuable. This was the position commonly called the Devil's Advocate. When the Catholic Church was considering whether to make someone a saint, they would investigate his life and works, reports of miracles performed and so on. They would appoint someone whose role it was to put the case against making him a saint. He'd have to find all the evidence and all the arguments he could to say why the person was not worthy of sainthood. Even if he really hoped the person would be made a saint, it was his duty to argue against it.

I think this was such a good idea that every committee should have its own devil's advocate; every Cabinet, every senior management team, every school's staff meeting. It would be that person's job to argue against whatever was proposed. If everyone else agreed with a proposal, if it was obviously the right thing to do, it would be especially important for the devil's advocate to make the best possible case against it. It's the best way of ensuring that all possible objections are considered, that all possible snags are addressed. It can even mean that some terrible mistakes are avoided.

I have often taken on the role of devil's advocate myself. It has not been too difficult for me as I often find that I do disagree with most people anyway, and I enjoy a good argument. I often find it intellectually stimulating to see how good a case I can make on behalf of some historical villain, or against some hero. Of course, it only works if you use evidence and sensible arguments, not just assertions, repetitions or aggression.

I'd recommend some of you to think about becoming devil's advocates. It can be great fun as well as very useful. You have to be a bit thick-skinned and prepared for people to be frustrated or annoyed by you. But sometimes you'll convince them that you're right, or you may win their respect even if you don't manage to persuade them. No one really respects a 'yes-man'!

Clergymen usually begin their sermons with a short quotation. I am going to end this talk with one. It alludes to Daniel, who the Bible tells us was put into a den of lions because he refused to bow down and worship a golden idol like everyone else. It comes from Philip P. Bliss's hymn, 'Dare to Be a Daniel':

> Dare to be a Daniel.
> Dare to stand alone.
> Dare to have a purpose firm,
> Dare to make it known.

Breadth and Depth

I'd like to put two ideas to you today that I hope you will think about. The first is this: that now and again we should all try to look at things from a different perspective, and question things we may have taken for granted. The more things are taken for granted by everyone, the more, perhaps, we need to question them.

One of the most famous English women of the Middle Ages was Mother Julian of Norwich. She was a woman of great intellect and learning, who wrote a very influential book called *Revelations of Divine Love*. Mother Julian was a recluse; she had shut herself away from the world to devote herself to prayer. People nowadays are not sympathetic to that; it seems selfish, even cowardly. The way to help others is to get out into the world and be active. I am certainly not drawn to shut myself away in a cell; I like to be out in the fresh air as much as possible, walking, running, sailing, kayaking or travelling. The interesting thing about reading what Mother Julian wrote, however, is that she does not come across as peculiar or out of touch but rather a warm human being who became a respected spiritual counsellor. Without being tempted to adopt her way of life, I can see that it has value.

Mother Julian's life seems to us terribly narrow, and we all know that what everyone should do is broaden their experience. Everything seems to be telling us to do so and making it easy for us to achieve. We can travel to all parts of the world without much difficulty; we can eat the food of many nations without leaving our neighbourhood; the school curriculum is very wide and there is often pressure to make it wider. How many subjects do you study? Twelve? Thirteen? If you had been to a grammar school 300 hundred years ago you would have probably studied just two, Latin and Greek, day after day, year after year. Television and computers widen your experience further. It would seem foolish to question the benefits of all this, and on the whole I wouldn't do so. However, since our time, energy and interest are not unlimited, it is worth asking whether we are trying to spread ourselves too widely. Are we sacrificing depth for the sake of breadth? That is the second of the two ideas I said I wanted you to think about.

Some years ago I watched two television programmes which have a bearing on this. One was from a series called *Wicker's World*. It showed a number of wealthy people who had sold their homes and were spending all their time on a luxury liner cruising around the world (they actually lived on the liner). In a literal sense they had broadened their horizons as much as anyone could; they were going to spend the rest of their lives travelling to every part of the world. Yet, as Alan Wicker interviewed them, the overwhelming impression was how shallow they all were. They seemed flat and boring; none of them said anything profound, interesting or amusing. When the ship docked in some exotic port many of the passengers did not even bother to disembark; it was enough just to tick if off the list of places to visit.

The other television programme was about a poor peasant in Italy. His vista was not as restricted as Mother Julian's. However, it wasn't very much wider. The programme followed him on a half-mile walk (or, I suppose I should say, a one kilometre walk) from his home to the other end of the village where he had a small plot of land. He did this walk, and of course the return journey, every day; he never went anywhere else. Throughout his life – and he was now in his seventies – he had never been outside the village. Yet he was a most interesting character. He was very observant and talked about the plants, insects, birds and animals he saw on his walk. He talked about the changes he noticed from day to day and season to season. He had shrewd insights into people and the world. Even though he was restricted to this kilometre range, he was a far more interesting person, in fact far more of a human being, than those who could travel the whole world.

In case anyone draws the wrong conclusion from this talk, let me emphasise that I am not recommending that you narrow your horizons and live within an area of a kilometre or half a mile. I have certainly never felt the urge to do that myself; quite the opposite. What I am suggesting is that breadth alone is not enough; we need depth as well. We need to get beneath the surface – of the world about us, of ourselves, of life.

RELIGIOUS TALKS

The Persian Carpet

One of the saddest statistics published each year is the number of people who have committed suicide. The number is always large, usually increasing, and consistently includes a larger proportion of young men than other groups. For the most part they are not people with painful or incurable diseases, or crippling disabilities, or people living in fear or hunger, but people with everything to look forward to. So why do they do it? Why take such an irrevocable step?

There are no doubt many reasons, but it seems that for most people it is because life seems pointless, meaningless. They cannot see any plan or pattern to their own life or to life in general. (It is interesting, by the way, to note that suicides go down in times of great hardship and danger, like wartime, perhaps because everyone can see a clear purpose then: survival or victory.)

By contrast, some of the people who have no doubts at all about the meaning of life in general, or about their own destiny, can be intolerant and ruthless. They probably won't commit suicide, but they may cause a great deal of misery to others.

So what is the answer, if seeing no pattern is dangerous and seeing an absolutely clear pattern is dangerous?

One of my favourite writers on religious subjects is C.S. Lewis. He wrote many books for children, but he also wrote a lot for adults. Quite often I've read something of his and thought, 'I should have realised that all along,' or even 'That's just what I've always thought, but haven't been able to express clearly.'

In one of his books he tells of a visit to a carpet factory in Persia, as Iran used to be called. Persian carpets are reckoned to be about the best in the world, with beautiful and intricate patterns on them. A dozen or so weavers were sitting on a long bench facing a huge roll of carpet – or rather canvas – which was pulled up very slowly as they each wove their wool through the square of canvas directly in front of them. What intrigued Lewis most was that they were all facing the back of the carpet, so they could not see the beautiful patterns they were weaving. All they could see were the rough ends of pieces of wool, a mass of colours with no distinct lines. It didn't matter however; they knew what they had to do on their piece of canvas. As long as they did that properly all would be well. It would only be when the carpet was finished that they would go round to the other side and see the whole thing. Then they would see just how beautiful the design was and how essential their own part had been. Whether they had worked in the centre or on the edge didn't matter; it was all necessary to make the whole thing right.

C.S. Lewis saw this as a metaphor for life. We are all like the carpet weavers and the square of rough canvas in front of us is our lifespan. As we work away at it, it seems a blur of colours and ragged ends without distinct shapes. We cannot, and should not, expect to see the design clearly, but we should trust that there is a design and a designer. And we all know what we have to do in our section of canvas; our consciences tell us. Like the weavers, we should feel confident that as long as we do what we should, we shall be contributing to the overall design. Confident also that when we eventually go round to the other

30

side – that is, when we die – we shall see how essential our part was to make the whole thing perfect, as the designer intended, whether it was in the centre or on the edge.

All of your teachers hope that all of you will have lives of happiness, success, fulfilment. However, just by the law of averages we know this will not be so. Some of you, perhaps most at one time or another, will face great sadness, disappointment or despair. If at these times you can remember the carpet weavers and realise that, although everything in front of you looks a rough and shapeless blur, there is a pattern to it which you will eventually see, it may help you to keep going, doing what you know is the right thing.

Lilies of the Field

I hope that some of you respond to the sound of words, and that you remember certain phrases or sentences because they somehow strike a chord with you. Quite a few phrases resonate with me, either because they are especially clear or beautiful or powerful. It helps if I agree with what they say, but that's not essential. For instance, I have always remembered a line from Milton's *Paradise Lost*, which I read about 45 years ago. In the poem Satan says, ''Tis better to rule in Hell than serve in Heaven.' I totally disagree with that sentiment, which can lead – indeed which frequently has led – to all sorts of evil, but it is a very powerful line.

There are many wonderfully memorable phrases in the Bible, or at least in the authorised King James version. In his sermon on the mount, Christ says:

> Consider the lilies of the field, how they grow; they toil not, neither do they spin. And yet I say to you that even Solomon in all his glory was not arrayed like one of these.
>
> Matthew, 7:28–29

That is one of my favourite short passages. The phrase 'even Solomon in all his glory' particularly has a ring to it for me. A few lines further on there is another powerful and slightly mysterious-sounding sentence: 'Sufficient unto the day is the evil thereof'. I shall come back to that passage in a few minutes, but put those thoughts to one side for now.

Most of us like to think we are being independent-minded and original. I expect your teachers have often told you to think for yourself, to express your own ideas. I wonder, however, how many of us are ever really original. I don't mean whether we wear certain clothes because we know our parents won't approve, but whether we look at our lives from a totally different angle, whether we question things everyone takes for granted. A few years ago on Radio 4 (my favourite station, as it's not spoiled by pop music) I heard a man talking about his proposed trip round the world, walking as much as possible, either wearing or carrying in his rucksack everything he possessed. He was thereby challenging two of the major preoccupations of most people: possessing all they can and being in easy communication with everyone they know. Come to think of it, he was also challenging a third preoccupation of many people: making life as easy and comfortable as possible. What a contrast he would make, as he strode over mountains and through wildernesses, with those people who cannot walk 100 yards down the road without speaking to half-a-dozen friends on their mobile phone, before they catch the bus to travel two stops home so that they can sit in front of the television for a few hours. How much freer that young man was going to be.

I remember someone once asking this about possessions, 'Do you possess them or do they possess you?' Perhaps I could ask this about modern communications, 'Do they keep you in touch with others, or out of touch with yourself?' I am not advising you all to throw away all your possessions and walk round the world, or saying that I'm tempted to do so, but I do think it was an admirable, brave and noble thing that young man did, and that we would all gain a lot, and probably be better people, if we tried to be a bit more like him and questioned some of the things on which we have become dependent.

Perhaps some of you have already seen a connection between these thoughts and one of my quotations earlier on. King Solomon was one of the wealthiest rulers of the ancient world, living in splendour and magnificence, with all the possessions anyone could want, yet, says Christ, simple wild flowers have more beauty than he had.

This is the time to read the whole passage from St Matthew's gospel from which the quotation comes:

Therefore I say unto you, Take no thought for your life, what ye shall eat, or what ye shall drink; nor yet for your body, what ye shall put on. Is not the life more than meat, and the body than raiment?

Behold the fowls of the air: for they sow not, neither do they reap, nor gather into barns; yet your heavenly Father feedeth them. Are ye not much better than they?

Which of you by taking thought can add one cubit unto his stature?

And why take ye thought for raiment? Consider the lilies of the field, how they grow; they toil not, neither do they spin.

And yet I say unto you, That even Solomon in all his glory was not arrayed like on of these.

Wherefore, if God so clothe the grass of the field, which today is, and tomorrow is cast into the oven, shall he not much more clothe you, O ye of little faith?

Therefore take no thought, saying, What shall we eat? or, What shall we drink? or, Wherewithal shall we be clothed?

(For after all these things do the Gentiles seek:) for your heavenly Father knoweth that ye have need of all these things.

But seek ye first the kingdom of God, and his righteousness; and all these things shall be added unto you.

Take therefore no thought for the morrow: for the morrow shall take thought for the things of itself. Sufficient unto the day is the evil thereof.

Matthew, 7:25–34

As I understand it, there are three important lessons in this passage, all clearly connected: one, the simplicity and beauty of nature, which I've already touched on; two, that God knows what we need and will provide it; three, that we should take no thought for tomorrow, for how we are going to make a living. This third lesson is a hard one.

Most teachers, and I am sure all of your parents, are always trying to persuade you to think more about the future: your exams, your options, your careers, for example. Common sense tells us the same; we shouldn't just live for today. So can Christ's words be reconciled with common sense? If they cannot, I don't see that as a problem. Christ often challenges his hearers to look at things in a totally new way, so that they have to question and re-evaluate their lives. He often says things that are staggeringly original, but perhaps his words can be reconciled to our idea of common sense. Perhaps he's not so much saying 'don't plan for the future' as 'don't worry about the future, don't be frightened about what might happen'. That, surely, must be good advice; however much we may plan or prepare for the future, anything may happen tomorrow which we cannot foresee and which we have no control over. So what is the point of worrying

35

today on account of something that may or may not happen tomorrow?

I read somewhere that brave men die once and cowards die many times. What the writer meant was that by fearing and worrying about death, the coward suffers much of the pain of dying over and over again. Far better to leave it until it actually happens. 'Sufficient unto the day is the evil thereof.'

Calming the Storm

For all my life – or at least for as long as I can remember – I've been interested in the sea; indeed I've felt drawn to it. I love looking at it, walking beside it, swimming in it, sailing on it; I love boats, lighthouses, sea cliffs, the smell of the sea, everything about it. So it is not surprising that the parts of the Bible that most immediately grab my attention are the passages about the sea. There aren't that many of them, for the Jews were primarily a pastoral and farming people, but they are all pretty dramatic: Noah's ark, Moses crossing the Red Sea, Jonah and the whale, for example. In the very first few lines of the Bible a powerful image of the sea is conjured up in these words: '...and darkness was upon the face of the deep. And the Spirit of God moved upon the face of the waters.' (Genesis, 1:2)

I think it is worth noting that the first people Jesus chose as his disciples were fishermen, while the New Testament records him performing several miracles at sea. I am going to read the account of one of these (from the Authorised – or King James – version of the Bible, which I think sounds far better than any other translation) and then say a few words about it.

This is St Mark's account:

And the same day, when the even was come, he saith unto them, Let us pass over unto the other side.

And when they had sent away the multitude, they took

him even as he was in the ship. And there were also with him other little ships, And there arose a great storm of wind, and the waves beat the ship, so that it was now full.

And he was in the hinder part of the ship asleep on a pillow: and they awake him, and say unto him, Master, carest thou not that we perish?

And he arose, and rebuked the wind, and said unto the sea, Peace, be still. And the wind ceased, and there was a great calm.

And he said unto them, Why are ye so fearful? How is it that ye have no faith?

And they feared exceedingly, and said one to another, What manner of a man is this, that even the wind and the sea obey him?

Mark, 4:35–41

I like this partly because it's a very good short story. It's worth reading even if you think it's pure fiction. In only 165 words there is action, atmosphere, drama and a shrewd insight into character. I like the way the disciples become resentful towards Jesus for sleeping through the storm. You can pick up their panic in the few words they say. If any of you have been in a storm at sea, or in any difficult situation, it can be really irritating if you are in a bit of a panic and someone else is totally calm and unconcerned, as if they can't see how serious things are. I actually like to think that Jesus was just pretending to be asleep to test the others, smiling to himself at the state they were getting themselves into. The gospel doesn't say that though, so perhaps it's an unworthy thought on my part.

The story can, however, be understood on a deeper level as well. Some people see it as a metaphor: in life we often meet turbulence, physical, mental or emotional storms. These can panic us and threaten to sink us, but if we realise that God is in control of everything we will calm down, lose our fear and survive. That seems to me a true and very powerful message.

It is equally true, however, that St Mark did not intend us to understand the story as a metaphor, or at least not just as a metaphor. He meant us to believe it literally; he wrote it as something that really happened. It is only if we can accept this that we will derive the full meaning, value and enjoyment from the passage. That does not mean that we cannot also appreciate it as a metaphor relevant to our everyday lives and enjoy it as a good story. They are not alternatives. We can enjoy it on three levels, or on two, or on just one. It is still worth reading.

Miracles

I suppose that few things put people off religion, or at least off Christianity, more than the Bible's accounts of miracles. A lot of people say that they agree with the moral teaching of Christianity and that they could believe in God, but that they cannot accept the miracles, which they see as just like fairy stories. Even a lot of religious people wish the miracles were not there and try to explain them away or find natural explanations for them. They think, probably correctly, that it would be easier to defend the faith nowadays if there were no accounts of miracles.

Not having studied theology, I don't claim to be any sort of expert; however, it does seem strange to me that anyone who can believe in a god who created everything – time and space as well as matter and life – out of absolutely nothing, finds it impossible to believe that He could, for instance, turn water into wine. The latter is a pretty small thing compared to the miracle of creation. Whether or not He did turn water into wine on a particular occasion, or cure some lepers on another, may be debatable, but whether or not He could do it is surely beyond question. My difficulty with miracles is not that they happened, but that they do not happen more often. Why doesn't God keep performing miracles to prevent terrible, undeserved suffering?

The best explanation of miracles that I have heard is that

given by C.S. Lewis, my favourite writer on religious questions. Lewis's view is that the purpose of Christ's miracles is to teach us about reality. They, or at least most of them, do not overrule nature, but tell us something about it which we overlook.

Let me give an example. In the gospels there is an account of Christ feeding five thousand people with five loaves and two fish. Impossible, say the sceptics. But what happens every year, in every sea and every river? A few fish become a huge number of fish by the natural method of laying eggs. And what happens in every cornfield? Enough corn to make a few loaves is sown in the ground and grows into enough corn to make thousands of loaves. What Christ is in fact saying is, 'Look, every year God performs these great miracles of increase and you take it for granted and fail to see His hand behind it. What I have done is the same thing, on a smaller scale and speeded up, before your eyes, but it is the same power behind both events.' Lewis points out that the miracle is in God's style: a few fish become a lot of fish, snakes don't become fish and stones don't become bread. (That, incidentally, was one of the devil's temptations rejected by Christ.) The water into wine follows the same pattern. Every year vines drink up water from the ground and produce grapes. When these are picked more water is added and in time it becomes wine. At Cana Christ just speeded up the change.

The healing miracles, claims Lewis, are not really different. For the most part our bodies heal themselves when they are sick or injured; medicine or treatment stimulates the process or removes obstructions but doesn't actually cure. God's power is behind the natural process just as it is behind Christ's healing.

Some miracles, of course, do not fit into this pattern: walking on water, calming the storm, raising the dead. These things don't happen naturally. What Lewis says is that these are a foretaste of what will happen after our resurrection; we shall be in a new relationship with nature, no longer at its mercy. These miracles are prophecies, whereas the others are reminders.

I shall end by quoting a couple of sentences taken from one of Lewis's sermons, *Miracles*, found in a book of his works entitled *God in the Dock*:

> One of their [the miracles'] chief purposes is that men, having seen a thing done by personal power on the small scale, may recognise when they see the same thing done on the larger scale, that the power behind it is also personal – is indeed the very same person who lived among us 2,000 years ago. The miracles in fact are a retelling in small letters of the very same story which is written across the whole world in letters too large for some of us to see.

Temptations

Many people give up something during Lent, which is a fairly feeble modern version of the serious fasting that used to take place. The idea was in part to remind people of the 40 days Christ fasted in the wilderness.

As well as fasting, the Bible tells us that Christ was tempted by the devil. This is St Matthew's account, from the Authorised, or King James, version which I much prefer to more modern translations:

And when he had fasted forty days and forty nights, he was afterward an hungered.

And when the tempter came to him, he said, If thou be the Son of God, command that these stones be made bread.

But he answered and said, It is written, Man shall not live by bread alone, but by every word that proceedeth out of the mouth of God.

Then the devil taketh him up into the holy city, and setteth him on a pinnacle of the temple,

And saith unto him, If thou be the Son of God, cast thyself down: for it is written, He shall give his angels charge concerning thee: and in their hands they shall bear thee up, lest at any time thou dash thy foot against a stone.

Jesus said unto him, It is written again, Thou shalt not tempt the Lord thy God.

43

Again, the devil taketh him up into an exceeding high
mountain, and showeth him all the kingdoms of the world,
and the glory of them;

And saith unto him, All these things will I give thee, if
thou wilt fall down and worship me.

Then saith Jesus unto him, Get thee hence, Satan: for it
is written, Thou shalt worship the Lord thy God, and him
only shalt thou serve.

Then the devil leaveth him, and, behold, angels came
and ministered unto him.

Matthew, 4:2–11

I can remember that when I first heard that story as a boy, I
half thought – although I knew I shouldn't – that Jesus should
have taken all the kingdoms of the world, as he could have
ruled them all justly and done so much good. I know that even
today if I were given these three temptations that would be the
one that would be the problem. I think I'd be okay at resisting
the other two, certainly the second one, but I'd be seriously
tempted by the third. And I could produce a number of reasons
to justify giving in: I could do a much better job than most of
the world's leaders and make the world a better and happier
place. However, I suppose that many of the worst tyrants in
history started out wanting to do good. Getting power was the
means to a good end, but somewhere along the way power
itself became the end, and the good intentions were cast aside.
They had not noticed the condition for getting power: 'Fall
down and worship me,' said the devil. Someone once said that
the only people who can be trusted with power are those who
don't seek it. I think there's a lot in that.

Is this story of interest just because it concerns Christ? After all,
none of us is likely to be faced with those actual temptations. But

each of these temptations can be easily 'translated' into one we all face, sometimes on a daily basis. Turning the stones into bread is the temptation to put material things first: food, money, possessions. Jumping off the temple is the temptation to show off, to win admiration or popularity by doing something we shouldn't, whether it is morally wrong, dangerous or just silly. And the temptation to gain the kingdoms of the world may be the desire for promotion, say, or for leadership of a team or club. There is nothing wrong with those ambitions in themselves, but if the price is to cheat, lie or denigrate a rival, then we are doing what we know to be wrong. We are in fact doing the equivalent of falling down and worshipping the devil.

Leadership

I have always been interested in questions of leadership and authority, and while it is perhaps more usual and more acceptable, especially among young people, to criticise and challenge authority, my sympathies have usually been on its side. This is partly because it has always seemed to me that without some sort of leadership or authority a group of people is unlikely to achieve anything worthwhile, and partly because exercising leadership or authority is pretty difficult. I have no doubt that your parents sometimes find it difficult to get you to do things you don't want to do, no matter how beneficial or necessary they are. How much more difficult to exercise authority over 30 people in a class, several hundreds in a school, thousands in an army or millions in a country.

What especially fascinates me is how some people exercise real authority with a minimal recourse to force. I remember Mr Hutchings at my secondary school, the teacher who had far and away the best discipline I have ever seen. He would walk into a classroom, the hall or the dining room and everyone would immediately fall silent and stand, or sit still. Yet he never raised his voice and never punished anyone. (He did once say I was in detention, but then let me off ...)

One of my heroes in history is Admiral Nelson. Apart from being very good at winning battles and saving the country from invasion, he was a great leader of men. For the most part the sailors on his ships were devoted to him, and they were a very tough lot, many of them the dregs of society. Navy life was very hard in those days, with brutal punishments, but Nelson resorted to these far less than other captains. He won his men's admiration by his personality and by exposing himself to the same dangers they faced.

King Henry VIII was a very different sort of person: selfish, a bully, a bit of a tyrant perhaps. He certainly had no qualms about punishing and executing people. Yet in his reign there was no police force in England, no standing army, only a tiny professional force of bodyguards. He nevertheless dominated the country, largely by his strong personality and the aura of kingship.

Three hundred years ago there was a great king of France, Louis XIV, who kept the country in submission by dazzling it with his magnificence. He built a vast palace and lived in such splendour that no one else, however rich or powerful, could come near to rivalling him. Everyone could see that the king was a being far above them, on a completely different level. It wasn't a style of leadership that most of us would sympathise with today, and it cost a vast amount which put up the taxes, but it was better than the civil wars that preceded Louis' reign. It was also vastly better than the concentration camps and mass executions employed by some more recent leaders, like Hitler and Stalin, as a way of keeping order.

Living in such style may not have been much fun for the king himself. The idea worked because the king was on show nearly all the time: crowds of noblemen would be in his bedroom when he got up in the morning and crowds of people would be in the passages and on the stairs of the palace (which in those unhygienic days made it smell pretty awful) awaiting his appearance. So much ceremony surrounded his meals (which people would watch) that he probably never ate hot food, and the palace could be so cold that at times, it is said, the wine froze in his glass.

I find all this very interesting, but is it the best way for leaders to behave? Jesus's style of leadership could hardly have been more different. He made his views on leadership clear in a very graphic way to his followers at the Last Supper. He washed his disciples' feet. That was a low and demeaning job, so much so that at first St Peter refused to let his feet be washed. It would not be a very pleasant thing to do nowadays, but 2,000 years ago when streets were not paved, when animals were carrying things up and down the road, and when most people wore open sandals or had bare feet, it would have been a lot worse. It would not just have been dust and mud on their feet. In big households washing the guests' feet was a task for the very lowest slaves or servants. After Christ has washed his disciples' feet he said this:

> Know ye what I have done to you? Ye call me Master and Lord: and ye say well; for so I am.
>
> If I then, your Lord and Master, have washed your feet; ye also ought to wash one another's feet.
>
> For I have given you an example, that ye should do as I have done to you.
>
> John, 13:12–15

What he is saying is that true leadership means setting a good example and attending to the needs of your followers. A real leader says 'come' not 'go'.

Frogs in a Bucket of Milk

A large bucket half full of milk was left outside a cowshed one night and three frogs jumped into it and couldn't jump out. There was nothing firm from which they could spring up and the sides were too slippery to grip on to.

One of the frogs gave up straightaway in despair, sank to the bottom and drowned. Another one struggled to jump out for a few minutes, but thinking it was hopeless, gave up and also sank and drowned. But the third frog carried on jumping up as much as he could, each time falling back into the milk. He kept this up for hour after hour all through the night, and each time he jumped he said, 'God help me.' In the morning he was still in the bucket, still alive, and lying exhausted on a mound of butter. His constant jumping had churned the milk into butter. The butter provided a firm enough platform for the frog to jump out of the bucket once he'd got his strength back and so hop off safely.

Now this story, as I'm sure you've realised, doesn't actually tell us anything about frogs. It is a sort of animal fable, one that I understand is used by teachers of Islam, and it tells us about prayer. It tells us three things about prayer, which I think all the world's great religions would agree with.

The first thing is that you should persevere in prayer and never give up, no matter how hopeless the situation may seem. The two frogs that lost hope and gave up, died. The one who kept asking for God's help, lived.

The second thing is that God often answers our prayers in ways we don't expect. Perhaps the frog hoped that God would give him a burst of super-strength that would enable him to jump out of the bucket in one huge leap. Perhaps he hoped for a miraculous hand to come down from the sky, pick him up and place him safely on the ground. What he could never have expected or imagined is that the milk would be turned into something solid enough for him to jump out with his own strength.

The third thing the story teaches – and I think this is the most important thing – is that prayer has to be accompanied by action. The frog didn't just lie back and ask for God's help; he kept jumping. Now I am not suggesting that when you say your prayers you should jump up and down like a frog. I think the headmaster would have something to say if we all did that a little later in this assembly. However, we have to do something to bring about the things we pray for. We shouldn't leave it all to God. For example, I think it is a very good idea to pray for success in exams, but you need to do the revision as well. If someone you love is ill you should pray for them, but you should also visit them in hospital, or do something for them that they cannot do for themselves. If you hear about a terrible disaster in the world, it's good to pray for the victims, but accompany your prayers with some action, even if you can do no more than put 10p in a collecting tin.

I've heard some people say: 'If God is so great, he can put everything right without us having to do anything or having to pray, so why do we need to bother?' I'd look at it in a different way and say that through our prayers and actions God is allowing us to cooperate with him in bringing about his purposes, which is actually a huge privilege and, when you think about it, a huge compliment.

The Bible: What's it All About?

Some years ago I saw a film called *Alfie*. It began (or perhaps ended, I forget which) to the words of a song 'What's It All About Alfie?' You'll be relieved to hear that I do not intend to sing it now. In any case, neither the song nor the film is relevant to this assembly, but I think the question is a good one to ask about the Bible. What's it all about?

I suppose that most people, if asked that question, would be able to answer that it was about God, or religion, or Jesus, or the ancient Hebrews. And no doubt many, though perhaps an ever-decreasing number, would remember some particular events it records. However, I expect many would find it difficult to explain what it was about in the way they could describe what a film or a novel was about. Nor is that surprising, as the Bible is a very long book. In fact, it is not really a book at all, but a collection of books of different types, written by different people over many centuries. The word 'bible' comes from the Latin *biblioteca*, which means library. It is perhaps better to regard the Bible as a library containing books of history, prophecy and poetry, for example, than as a single book. It may, therefore, seem pointless to expect to find any sort of coherent theme running through it, though not to those of us who believe all the books are inspired by God in some way.

What I propose to do in under five minutes is to explain what

I see the Bible as being all about. Or rather, not *all* about, but the core theme running through it. So here goes, start the clock.

God alone has no beginning, has always existed and He created everything else out of nothing: time, space, the universe, matter, energy, life, everything. He made people more like Him than any other created things, with some of His characteristics, like reason, free will and a moral sense.

He hoped people would freely do what was right, but very early on they deliberately did what they knew to be wrong. This, and the sense of guilt it produced, caused a gulf between them and God, a separation from Him. This is what the Church calls original sin and we all inherit it; it is in our genes, if you like, part of our DNA. Because of this we, unlike – as far as we know – anything else in creation, live with a dissatisfaction, a restlessness, a want of harmony. We know things are not as they should be; we are like square pegs in round holes. The theme of the Bible is the bridging of this gulf between us and God, the ending of this separation.

People have tried all sorts of things to end this state of affairs, to make them right with God, or the gods. They have tried magic; human and animal sacrifices; denying themselves all the comforts and pleasures most people enjoy; drawing up long lists of rules, often petty or pointless, to make life difficult and then obeying them to the letter. Others – and here I am drawing on history in general rather than the Bible directly, although I think the points are at least implied in it – who may or may not have believed in God, have tried to dull or overcome this sense of dissatisfaction by wallowing in luxury, by drugs of one sort of another, by the relentless pursuit of wealth or, most dangerous of all, by the pursuit of unlimited power over others. None of the attempts have worked in the long run, often not even in the short term. They try to blot out reality, rather than get to grips with it.

The crucial point the Bible makes is that people cannot achieve this bridging of the gap on their own. So God took the initiative. He called Abraham to a special destiny and revealed Himself bit by bit to him and his descendants by miracles, by the Ten Commandments, through the history of the Hebrews, through the teaching of the prophets. By stages people came to understand more and more what God was like and how they were meant to live. Yet still more needed to be done to bridge the gap, to restore the lost harmony.

In the person of Jesus Christ, God entered the world in a direct way; he was a human being like us, yet at the same time the Son of God, or God the Son. He was the bridge. In the way that he lived and in what he taught, he showed us what God was like and what we should be like. By his crucifixion, resurrection and ascension he took on the suffering due to all of us, overcame death and took humanity back to God, healing or reversing the separation, making possible the restoration of the lost harmony. He then sent the Holy Spirit to inspire his followers and lead them into the fullness of truth, founding the Christian Church, which is in a mysterious way the body of Christ on earth. The disciples began confidently to spread his teaching and to explain the meaning of all that had happened, not just to the descendants of Abraham, but to everyone.

The last book of the Bible, Revelation, is very difficult to understand, but the key points it makes are that there will be a judgement for everyone, that the universe will come to an end and that there will be a new and perfect existence for those judged righteous.

Well, my watch tells me that that took four and a half minutes.

It has not been my purpose, and indeed it is not my right nor in my power, to persuade you that the Bible is true, but to describe what, in my view, it is about. I'm sure that even the most militant atheists recognise that the Bible has been very important in our history and culture, and that everyone should have some idea of what is says. Some Christians believe everything in it is true in a completely literal way, virtually dictated by God to the writers; others believe that while some of it is literally, historically true, other parts tell truths in other ways, through myth, for instance. I hope they would all agree with my brief summary of its theme. Even more, I hope I have told you nothing wrong or heretical. However, as I've had no training in theology or biblical studies, if your priest or pastor or Religious Education teacher tells you something different, you will do better to believe them than me.

Gospel Trivia

I am going to read a short account from St John's gospel of one of the things Jesus did and then give you some of my thoughts on it.

> And the scribes and Pharisees brought unto him [Jesus] a woman taken in adultery; and when they had set her in the midst,
>
> They say unto him, Master, this woman was taken in adultery, in the very act.
>
> Now Moses in the law commanded us, that such should be stoned: but what sayest thou?
>
> This they said tempting him, that they might have to accuse him. But Jesus stooped down, and with his finger wrote on the ground, as though he heard them not.
>
> So when they continued asking him, he lifted up himself, and said unto them, He that is without sin among you, let him first cast a stone at her.
>
> And again he stooped down and wrote on the ground.
>
> And they which heard it, being convicted by their own conscience, went out one by one, beginning at the eldest, even unto the last: and Jesus was left alone, and the woman standing in the midst.
>
> When Jesus had lifted up himself, and saw none but the woman, he said unto her, Woman, where are those thine accusers? Hath no man condemned thee?

She said, No man, Lord. And Jesus said unto her, Neither do I condemn thee: go and sin no more.

John, 8:3–11

That story raises a number of important questions: Are we still bound by the laws of Moses? Should we show mercy to wrongdoers? How bad is adultery? (Note that Jesus says to the woman 'sin no more'; he doesn't say 'do what you like, it's your life'.) What were the scribes and Pharisees like? (After all, they were honest enough to accept that they had all sinned.) Actually, I am not going to talk about any of these issues, but about the one totally unimportant detail in the story.

When the woman is brought to Jesus he stoops down and writes in the dust on the ground with his finger. He does the same once he has delivered his opinion. There is no hint of what he wrote, so obviously that doesn't matter. I imagine he was just doodling rather than writing words. Nothing comes of it, whether words or doodles; it has no significance. So why is it included? Presumably because that is what happened. St John is writing down what he saw, or what someone else told him he saw. Perhaps Jesus was giving himself a little time to think what to say; perhaps, as a well-brought-up man, he was embarrassed at seeing the woman. Lots of us look down and fiddle with something if we're embarrassed.

If St John had invented the story he would not have included an unimportant detail. A modern novelist might do this, for the sake of realism, but 2,000 years ago people did not write in that way. If they had been inventing a story, they would have been far more likely to show the hero as decisive, giving an instant, wise judgement, not caught off guard and having to think about what to say.

There are other places in the gospels where something

unimportant is included. To me, these parts make the accounts authentic; they convince me that they are true. Do you remember the account of Christ's first miracle? At a wedding feast in Cana his mother comes to tell him that the wine has run out, so that he can do something about it. His reply shocked me when I first heard it as a boy. He said, 'Woman, what have I to do with thee? Mine hour is not yet come.' I knew that if I spoke to my mother like that, I'd be smacked. Even if the use of the word 'woman' like that would not have seemed rude then as it does now, Jesus clearly shows he is cross at being asked. I suppose he was enjoying the party with his friends and resented his mother butting in and implying that he should go and help the hosts.

Within a few minutes he does the right thing, as his mother knew he would. (I'm sure many of you are like that; show your annoyance but then think better of it and do what you've been asked. I know I am at times.) The point is, though, that this shows a very human reaction. If a writer in those days – or even perhaps today – were inventing a story about his hero, he wouldn't have put that in. He'd have had Jesus doing what was asked straightaway, speaking politely and gratefully to his mother, or not even having to be asked to do what was needed. He would not have shown him being irritated, abrupt and resisting his duty for a few minutes.

Some of you may like to look for other examples of this. Of course, it is not for me to say that you should believe what is in the gospels, but I hope you accept that the people who wrote them believed what they were writing. They were not inventing stories. They were reporting what they remembered seeing, or what others remembered. The books of the Bible are of different types and written in different ways. I'm referring specifically to the four gospels. The sort of thing I have drawn your attention to today is clearly not what is important about them. The things are trivial, but for that very reason they help to convince me that they are genuine.

The Hard Sayings of Jesus

I suppose that most of us, if we are honest with ourselves, would like a religion that gave us a lot of comfort and good feeling but that made no real demands on us. One that said in effect: As long as you are a reasonably decent person and help your friends and relations a little when they're in trouble, you can lead your own life and enjoy yourself. At the end of the day you'll be alright; if you've made mistakes or done anything bad it can be overlooked. Perhaps it will be like that, but none of the world's great religions say that it will. They all make demands on us; they all make it clear that we need to struggle against some of our desires and weaknesses, to make an effort to improve those parts of our character that are not as they should be. And we probably all realise that it must be so. If, let us say, you wanted to be a top footballer or athlete and your trainer said that you could carry on with your normal life, and not have to do any tiring exercise or give up any fattening foods, you might think 'this is good, much easier than I expected' for a few days, but you would soon realise that you would be in no shape to do well in the big match or the big competition. Or let us suppose you want to gain really good exam results. If your teachers said, 'Don't bother about homework, don't bother to read any books, don't come to lessons if you'd rather not. You're young, just enjoy yourself,' you would soon realise that however good it sounded it would not equip you to pass the exam. In the same way we are not going to be fit for eternal life, or even for a fulfilled life here and now, if we only do what is easy and enjoyable.

All the worthwhile religions tell us to do some things that are difficult. I don't know enough about religions other than Christianity to explain their teachings in a way that would be other than shallow or patronising; however, I know that Jesus said some very hard things. In a way nearly everything he said is hard. Some of the things are hard to put into practice, but not hard to approve of or accept as being right. For example, he said that we should love one another, love our neighbours and even love our enemies. That is terribly hard to do and often seems impossible. Yet most of us can see that it is right, that the world would be a much better place if everyone did it, that we would be better people if we could do it. Similarly with forgiving those who wrong us, or giving to those in need, turning the other cheek or walking the extra mile with someone. All very hard to do, though not so hard to believe. It is not to these sayings that I want to draw your attention today, but to the things Jesus said that are hard to believe, that seem to go against what we think is right.

Let me give you two examples of what I mean. St Matthew records that when Jesus was calling people to be his disciples, one man asked to be allowed to go and bury his father first. Jesus' reply was, 'Let the dead bury their dead,' (Matthew, 8:22). St Luke quotes Jesus as saying, 'If any man come to me and hate not his father, and mother, and wife, and children, and brethren, and sisters, yea, and his own life also, he cannot be my disciple,' (Luke, 14:26). Now what I find hard about those two sentences is not that it would be impossible to do what Jesus says, though it would be very hard, but that it would be wrong to do so. My conscience tells me that we should love our fathers, mothers etc., not hate them, and that we should carry out, not leave to others, our responsibilities to them, even once they have died. Since I claim to be a Christian, that creates a big problem for me. Can I possibly say that Jesus is wrong? If not, how do I solve the problem?

One solution, I suppose, would be to suppress my conscience and try to hate my nearest relations. But if we've been given consciences we're meant to obey them, not ignore them. Another solution would be to believe, or pretend to myself to believe, what Jesus said when I'm in church or talking about religion and to act on what I really think for the rest of the time. That would be hypocrisy, however, which I'm afraid is a bad fault that religious people are sometimes guilty of, and which probably puts more good people off religion than anything else. A third solution would be to say that I can't understand it, so I'll do what I think is right. If it hasn't been a problem for churchmen and theologians down the ages, there is no point in me worrying about it. I have sympathy with this view and think there is nothing shameful about admitting we don't know all the answers. And yet, if we've been given brains, we are surely meant to use them as far as we can, just as we are meant to use our consciences. Perhaps Jesus' words are not quite as difficult as they seem.

Jesus often looked at life from a different angle to other people in order to shake them out of their complacency, so that they re-evaluated their lives and their principles. Perhaps that is the explanation for his harsh words, to wake us all up to the fact that family affections and family duties are not all that matter, and that they should not always come first. What is more, Jesus wasn't a sort of walking philosophy of life; he was a real person who spoke to other real people. I don't think we should assume that everything he said was addressed to everyone in the world.

Some things were aimed at particular people. One man, for instance, was told to give all his possessions away, presumably because they meant too much to him; they were his fatal weakness. Others were told to be more prudent and worldly-wise, presumably for the opposite reason.

In the same way, some people care for no one beyond their family and will use their relatives as the reason, or excuse, for neglecting other duties or even for harming others. Some people who say that charity begins at home (true enough, in my opinion) really mean charity ends at home. These are the people who need to be told to think less of home. I think it quite likely that Jesus' harsh words were aimed at people like them, people whose family affections and duties were stifling them, holding them back from what they should be doing. Furthermore, we are not all called to live the same sort of life. Many religions, though not all, regard priests, monks and nuns as living not just valuable lives, but in some ways better lives than the rest of us. They do not, however, suggest we should all become priests, monks or nuns. They are the callings of a minority. Jesus no doubt understood that the people who were to start the Church, to spread it and lead it, needed to be single-minded, and totally committed; in following him they needed to be free of family ties. That doesn't mean that he thought we all should be.

If your priest or pastor says that I've got this wrong, listen to him or her. I am not a minister of religion and I haven't studied theology. I am not trying to persuade anyone to agree with me on this. What I have tried to do is twofold: firstly, I have tried to show that Jesus was not a sort of Father Christmas, giving us all presents and saying, 'Ho, ho, ho!' He made demands and said some hard things and we should not pretend otherwise. Secondly, I have tried to explain how I solve the problems some of these demands and words cause.

Holy Communion

Holy Communion is the most important service in the majority of Christian churches. It goes under various names – Mass, Eucharist, The Lord's Supper, as well as Holy Communion – but all the services, whatever else they do, commemorate what Christ did at his last supper with his disciples on the evening before his crucifixion. In case any of you are not familiar with what happened, Christ blessed some bread, broke it and gave it to the others to eat, saying, 'This is my body.' Then he gave thanks over a cup of wine and gave it to them to drink saying, 'This is my blood, which is shed for many for the forgiveness of sins.' At some times in the past Christians have not only argued over the exact meaning of those words but, to their shame, have fought and killed each other over it. I think, however, that most would accept that in some mysterious way Christ is present at Holy Communion, in a different way from how he was, or is, present elsewhere.

I'd like to explain in about five minutes what Holy Communion means to me. Not being a theologian, I am not going to get into the argument all the fighting has been about. In any case, I'm not sure that we can be very exact about religious questions; they are not the same as problems in Maths or Chemistry, for example. Perhaps religion fits somewhere between Maths and Science on the one hand and Art and Poetry on the other; we need to draw on the disciplines and insights of both to get to the heart of it. What I would say about Holy Communion is that it demonstrates how the ordinary can be extraordinary.

Let me explain what I mean. You can't have any food much more ordinary than bread; for much of the world it is, and always has been, the most basic food, the staff of life. Wine may seem a bit special to us, but in the past when there was no tea, coffee, Coke or drinking chocolate, and when water was often impure, wine and beer were the ordinary things to drink. So both bread and wine were pretty ordinary, yet at Holy Communion they bring to us, in some mysterious way, the presence of Christ, the Son of God, or God the Son. Nothing could be more extraordinary than that. Yet at the same time they remain ordinary: they still look, feel and taste like bread and wine; they still have the chemical composition of bread and wine.

As I think about it, this seems to be very much the way Christianity tells us that God works. What could be more ordinary than water? Yet it is with water at baptism that we become members of the Church in the first place. And look at the apostles and most of the saints: very ordinary people with their fair share of human weaknesses, who become very extraordinary when they are called by God. Interestingly they often, at the same time, remain ordinary on another level and keep their personalities, even their irritating traits and annoying habits.

Of course, the central mystery of Christianity bears out this same idea: a man who was fully human, living an ordinary childhood, eating, drinking, sleeping in the ordinary way, losing his temper at times, dying as fully as anyone else does, yet at the same time being the Son of God, God the Son. What could be more extraordinary?

Returning to the Holy Communion, it seems to me totally right that it has so central a place in the worship of the Church, for it puts before us, sacramentally, a fundamental truth of Christianity: that the ordinary becomes extraordinary when it is touched by the words, or the Word, of God.

TALKS FOR SIXTH-FORM ASSEMBLIES

Tradition

There are two bad things about having to take an assembly for the Sixth Form. One is that most of you probably not only don't want to be here, but also think you shouldn't have to be here at your age. The other is that you have sat through so many assemblies in your life that you have already decided you are going to be bored stiff. There are also, however, two good things about talking to you. Firstly you have, we trust, the intelligence and maturity of thought to follow a line of argument without me having to oversimplify it. Secondly, you can distinguish between fact and opinion, so I don't have to worry about indoctrinating you or using my position to influence you unfairly. You will be able to tell that I am giving you my opinion, not proven facts, and you will, I hope, accept that we are all entitled to our opinions.

What I am going to say is political in a fundamental way. It is not party political, though you may feel it has party implications. I am going to talk about something that is not of immediate interest to most people of your age. In fact, that is putting it mildly; it probably makes them 'switch off'. I am going to talk about tradition. I don't mean particular traditions, like Trooping the Colour or Black Rod knocking on the door of the House of Commons, but Tradition with a capital T. It means handing on, or handing down from one generation to another.

Human beings have a big problem: we know that we need to live in society for all sorts of reasons, including security, culture and prosperity, but we also want to pursue our own ends and look after our own interests, which sometimes conflict with society's. We are not like bees that live only for the hive, nor like those reptiles that live so completely for themselves that they will eat their own offspring if they can catch them. We therefore live with a tension; we are pulled in two directions. It seems to me that dealing with the tension, reconciling the demands of society with the rights of the individual, is the fundamental issue of politics and of history, at least of political history, which is what interests me most. It further seems to me that this issue breaks down into two questions: Where do we draw the line between the rights of society and the rights of the individual? How do we ensure that the individual accepts the interests of society when they seem to conflict with his or her own?

Let us look at the second of these questions first. How does society get people to pay their taxes, obey the laws, fight for the country perhaps, when they may not want to do any of these things? Every society will have to be able to use force as a last resort, whether imposing imprisonment, fines, expulsion or execution, for example. However, most of us would think force should be kept to a minimum and that the less it is needed the better. What about an appeal to reason or a reliance on people's good nature? These have been tried but sadly, though not unsurprisingly, they have not worked for long and with many people have not worked at all. Persuasion, propaganda, indoctrination (brainwashing) and bribery have all been tried and have all failed in the end. The late historian A.J.P. Taylor (who was, by the way, a left-winger, not by any means a Conservative) wrote in one of his essays that peaceful argument and government by consent were only possible on the basis of ideas common to all parties; and that these ideas had to spring from habit and from history. That is, they must come from tradition. History and our own experience show that it is easier to accept an obligation if it has always been an obligation, if it was an obligation for our parents and our grandparents, than if it is newly imposed. It is easier to accept an authority if it has always been there than if it is new. Tradition can make things seem part of the natural fabric of life, which we can accept without resentment and so without the need for force. That seems to me wholly good, far more important than worrying about whether they look modern or old-fashioned.

Turning now to the first of the two questions I suggested: Where do we draw the line between the rights of society and the rights of the individual? Throughout history people have come up with very different answers to this question. At one extreme, some have said that society is everything and the individual nothing. There were some societies like this is the ancient world, one of the best examples being Sparta. Weak babies were left to die on a cold hillside; only the strong would be of use to the state, the interests of the individual did not come into it. Modern, in some ways even more extreme, versions of the same idea, have been the Communist, Fascist and Nazi totalitarian systems. The individual was not even allowed his own thoughts. The Italian Fascist leader, Mussolini, once boasted that the people would be free only to dream; for all their waking lives they would be like cogs in the state machine. Fortunately, it did not work out like this, and these totalitarian systems have in the end collapsed, being incompatible with human nature or the human spirit.

At the other end of the spectrum are those who believe the individual is everything and should be free to do as he or she likes without having to consider society, the state, the government or any authority. Anarchists, extreme libertarians and extreme capitalists all get close to this. As indeed do some pupils in any school. I suppose the purest example would be the amoral criminal: he or she is concerned only with what he or she wants. Any such ideas if put into practice on a wide scale would, of course, make society impossible; it would degenerate into the law of the jungle.

Most of us would prefer to live in a society that fits somewhere between the two extremes, but that still leaves the problem of where to draw the line, of what is the right balance. Many countries, most nowadays, try to fix it with a written constitution. At some stage a group of people sit down and work out where it should be and try to ensure that it is difficult to change it. However, this seldom solves the problem as no one can foresee how society will develop and, in any case, we don't want the line to be always in the same place. For instance, during war or at a time of real national crisis or disaster, most of us would accept, would welcome, an increase in society's rights and powers. We'd give up some freedom in return for more security or help. When there is peace and prosperity, when everything is going well for us, we are likely to want more freedom and to resent society's demands and restrictions. How societies deal with this seems to me more a matter of trial and error, or growing experience, than of theory and planning. The handing on of this experience is Tradition. Customs, habits, institutions are the mechanisms by which it is transmitted.

A criticism often levelled at tradition is that it is an attempt to fossilise society, to freeze it in a past age and resist all change. I would say that this is by no means necessarily the truth, in fact very far from the truth. By not being written down in laws and codes, tradition has flexibility. It is like a river following on, with more and more streams flowing into it as time advances, yet still being the same river. Britain's form of government, its constitution, is more traditional than most countries', probably more than any other developed, industrialised country's. Yet, I am not shy of saying we have done pretty well, over a long period of time, in balancing the demands of society with the rights of the individual. The framework of tradition has allowed change without instability; evolution rather than revolution. Many countries that have discarded tradition and tried to base their constitutions on reason and high-minded principles have fared much worse. Some have lurched between tyranny and anarchy. Some have collapsed altogether. This does not surprise me. If you cut through the roots of a tree it may stand for a while, but it will crash at the first strong wind.

Objections to Religion

Recently someone said to me, 'My real objection to religion is that it is supposed to be about doing good, but it has been the cause of all the wars in the world.' I've heard that argument before and it never fails to annoy me. I admit that some wars have been caused by religion. For some wars religion has been one cause among many, while for others it has been the excuse or justification but not the real cause. But all of them? You do not have to think for more than half a minute to realise that is not true. Take these wars, in reverse chronological order: the Falklands War, the Korean War, the Second World War, the wars between Italy and Abyssinia and China and Japan in the 1930s, the First World War, the Boer War, the Zulu Wars, the American Civil War, the Napoleonic Wars. None of them were caused by religion. Or go back further into history: the Wars of the Roses, The Hundred Years War, the wars fought in the growth of the Roman Empire. I could go on, but I think I've proved the point. The sad thing is that I expect that when the man I referred to gets into another argument about religion, he will still use the same objection to it: the clear evidence to the contrary will not have shaken his prejudice, or his belief if you like. (I don't claim to have evidence to support all my beliefs; however, I trust that I would never cling to a belief that was contradicted by evidence.)

In this assembly I am going to look at a few other objections to religion. First a disclaimer: I am not trying to make anyone religious who isn't. I admit it would be a bonus if I did, but it is most unlikely and is, in any case, not my intention. My purpose is in fact to encourage you to discuss a whole range of issues on the basis of reason and evidence, not prejudice and assertion.

The silliest objection to religion that I ever heard was made by Nikita Khrushchev, a former leader of the former Soviet Union and clearly no fool in general. He was firmly against religion. He actually closed many churches that even the militant atheist (and mass-murderer) Stalin had allowed to reopen during the Second World War. After his government had put the first person ever into space, Khrushchev said he now had proof that there was no God, as this 'spaceman' (Yuri Gagarin) had seen that there was no one up there. Perhaps he was joking, though he didn't seem to be; perhaps he thought religious people were so stupid that they would be impressed by this 'proof' and abandon their faith. Perhaps he really believed what he said. I'm sure I don't have to persuade you of the weakness of Khrushchev's claim, whether or not you believe in God.

Many of the objections to religion are far stronger than that one and deserve to be considered seriously. It is a great mistake, whether in war, politics, religion or almost anything, to underestimate your opponents, to assume that anyone who disagrees with you must be stupid or ignorant or just prejudiced. One argument often voiced is that science has disproved religion, that religion was understandable as a way of explaining things when we did not actually know much about the world or the universe, but is redundant now that we do. Science may have disproved many religious notions – often, in fact, cultural ideas that have attached themselves to religion – but in essence religion and science are asking different questions. Science is trying to answer the question 'how?'

religion is trying to answer 'why?'. Many scientists, including one of the greatest, Einstein, believe, or believed, in God and most religious people accept the discoveries of science. It is more likely to be people with little understanding of either science or religion who think they are incompatible.

An argument that derives from a scientific approach is that religion has an evolutionary function: that it evolved within our ancestors to help them cope with the world and helped them survive, and that it therefore has no objective truth. It has even been suggested that there may be a 'religious gene' that some people have that predisposes them to be religious. There have indeed been some recent studies that indicated that religious people in general live longer, have better health and are happier than non-religious people. Unless we take a very crude view that God rewards believers in this way, it would seem to support the idea of evolutionary advantage. However, the conclusion to be drawn from it could just as easily be the opposite to the one suggested. After all, if something helps us survive or if our genes tell us we need something, that thing has a reality and a necessity, a truth if you like, rather than the opposite. So, for instance, we feel hunger because we need food and of course because there is such a thing as food. We feel pain because something has gone wrong with our body which we need to put right. If people feel a need to worship – and it seems that people in all cultures in all parts of the world since before civilisation have felt that need – that suggests to me that there is something to worship and that it is important to do so. I know it is not the same as food and I realise I haven't presented a tight argument, but that is the way my thoughts are going. Perhaps some of you could even help me out, or slap me down, over this.

Maybe the strongest objection to religion, or at least to the three Abrahamic religions, is the existence of suffering in the world. If God is both all-powerful and all-loving, why does He permit terrible, undeserved suffering? Some religions say that none is undeserved but is a punishment of wrongs committed in a previous life. Not believing in reincarnation, that is not a solution open to me. Others say there are two equal and opposite forces of good and evil, forever battling it out in the universe; suffering comes from the evil power. But that solution is not open to monotheists.

Fundamentally there are two sorts of suffering: that which comes from other people and that which comes from nature, such as earthquakes, floods, droughts and diseases. I don't find too much difficulty with the first sort; it derives from people's free will. If God gave us free will He accepted the possibility that we would make wrong, even evil, choices, as much as He hoped and intended that we should choose the good. Free will is essential to our humanity; without it we would be like robots or at least like those animals that cannot make moral choices. It is a sign of God's love, just as it is a sign of a parent's love when he or she lets a child go out alone for the first time. He or she hopes nothing will go wrong but accepts that risk comes with freedom, without which there could not be real development and fulfilment. It is hard to see how the other sort of suffering could be explained in a similar way, though there are people who have tried. Perhaps life, the world, the universe could not possibly exist without the things that lead to terrible, impersonal suffering. Perhaps even the most awful viruses have an essential role to play which we do not yet understand. It will be objected that if God is all-powerful He could have made it all different, so that the world didn't need such horrors. But even an all-powerful God cannot do absolutely anything. He cannot make two plus two equal five, because that is a contradiction in terms. Perhaps there could be no other possible universe.

I did say that I find this the strongest objection to religion. I know that I have not dealt adequately with it but I don't feel I can go any further with it at the moment. What we do know is that suffering is real, it is a fact of life; we cannot have life on any other conditions. I would add that nevertheless life is wonderful, a free gift that none of us has done anything to deserve.

Religious Truth

I believe that what Christianity teaches is true. I do not claim to put it into practice very well and I certainly do not think it makes me any better than non-Christians. However, I think it is true in a way that other beliefs are not. Perhaps it would be better to say that I think it is nearer the truth than other beliefs, religious or non-religious. A good argument that has been used against my position is that I only think this because I have been born and brought up a Christian, and that I would believe Islam to be true if I had been born and brought up a Muslim. Likewise, if I had been born a Jew, a Hindu or a Buddhist. Therefore there is no religious truth; it is all just a matter of opinion and upbringing. Now the first part of the argument is true; although for a few teenage years I called myself an atheist, I never seriously considered changing from Christianity to another religion and I expect the same is true for the vast majority of believers. People may drop out of the religion of their birth, but very few change to another. I do not, however, accept the second part of the argument, that there is therefore no religious truth, though it makes a strong point: all religions cannot be true but they can all be untrue. This is the problem I want to talk about today.

I suspect that I may have already turned some of you against this assembly: the atheists and agnostics because you fear you're going to be preached at about why you should be religious, and the followers of other religions because I seem to be plugging Christianity. Before the assembly is over I may have annoyed some Christians most of all because I seem to be letting the side down and diluting the more exclusive claims Christianity makes. However, you do not deserve to be sixth formers if you are not prepared to listen to a wide range of ideas and opinions.

To return to the problem: religious people believing their own faith to be true, but accepting, on the evidence and reason, that had they been born to other parents or in another country they might believe another faith to be true. Whatever else this problem does, it should make us all tolerant of other beliefs. We should not persecute anyone on the simple grounds that 'there but for the grace of God go I'. It is not the issue of tolerance that I want to pursue however, but the issue of truth.

Let me talk about my own experience for a minute, not because it's particularly interesting but because it makes it easier to explain my view. When I was about 17 I began to think more seriously about religion and to reject the atheism I had embraced three or four years earlier. As it happens, this had more to do with my study of history and the influence of a brilliant history teacher than with anything more narrowly religious, but that is by the way. Over the next few years I talked with and listened to some practising Christians, read some things and started going to church, occasionally at first. When I was 21 I became confirmed into the Church of England. I had not made any attempt to find out what other religions taught and to weigh up their comparative merits. The nearest I came to this, and it wasn't very near at all, was to wonder whether I should stay in the church of my birth or become a Roman Catholic.

Now, far from feeling guilty or apologetic about this, I think what I did was both natural and right. Coming from a Christian background and living in a Christian culture – far more true in the 1960s than today – it was easier and more reliable to explore spiritual questions by delving more deeply into Christianity than by reading up on all the world's religions and trying to decide which was the truest. The latter course would almost inevitably have been superficial (unless I spent nearly all my time on it) and any decision I came to may have had more to do with my tastes than anything deeper. I think exactly the same is true of people from Muslim, Jewish, Buddhist and Hindu backgrounds: if they want to understand more about God and spiritual matters they will do better to delve deeper into their own traditions than embark on a Cook's tour of all the others. Only much later will some of them be able to gain real insights from other religions, as opposed to a mere glimpse of their buildings, festivals and peculiarities.

I have heard of a sort of analogy used, I think, in Hinduism, which I find useful. The world is like a great mountain, at the summit of which is God. Round the base of the mountain are a number of villages that represent the nations or cultures of the world. From each village a path leads up the mountain to the summit. These paths are the religions of the world. Where they begin they are miles apart, out of sight of each other, but the higher they go, the nearer they get to the summit, the nearer they get to each other. When they reach the summit, of course, they meet. The same is true of the people who walk up the paths.

Now, I am not putting this before you as a truth you should believe. Apart from anything else, it seems to go against some of what the monotheistic religions, especially Christianity perhaps, teach. But I do find it a useful idea to think about. It does seem to give an insight into the pursuit of religious truth and how that can be reconciled with tolerance of, and respect for, those who are pursing the truth by a different path. Many sincere people find it difficult to do this. Also, it has some relevance to the claim I made earlier that it is best to seek greater spiritual understanding by starting from the tradition you were born and bred into. What is the best way for a person in one of the villages round the base of the mountain to reach the summit? To start walking up the path that leads from his village or to spend months or years walking round the base, looking at all the paths and trying to decide which of them will enable him to reach the top quickest?